These Are My Senses

KU-153-070

What Can I Smell?

Joanna Issa

Raintree is an imprint of Capstone Global Library Limited, a company incorporated in England and Wales having its registered office at 7 Pilgrim Street, London, EC4V 6LB – Registered company number: 6695582

www.raintreepublishers.co.uk
myorders@raintreepublishers.co.uk

Text © Capstone Global Library Limited 2015
First published in hardback in 2014
The moral rights of the proprietor have been asserted.

All rights reserved. No part of this publication may be reproduced in any form or by any means (including photocopying or storing it in any medium by electronic means and whether or not transiently or incidentally to some other use of this publication) without the written permission of the copyright owner, except in accordance with the provisions of the Copyright, Designs and Patents Act 1988 or under the terms of a licence issued by the Copyright Licensing Agency, Saffron House, 6–10 Kirby Street, London EC1N 8TS (www.cla.co.uk). Applications for the copyright owner's written permission should be addressed to the publisher.

Edited by Siân Smith
Designed by Richard Parker and Peggie Carley
Picture research by Tracy Cummins
Production by Victoria Fitzgerald
Originated by Capstone Global Library Ltd
Printed and bound in China by RR Donnelley Asia

ISBN 978 1 406 28371 6
18 17 16 15 14
10 9 8 7 6 5 4 3 2 1

British Library Cataloguing in Publication Data
A full catalogue record for this book is available from the British Library.

Acknowledgements
We would like to thank the following for permission to reproduce photographs: Corbis: Onoky/© Eric Audras, 9; Getty Images: Vetta/MariaPavlova, 19, 22 left; iStock: © Alija, 16, 20 left, © Stacey Newman, 5, 22 right; Shutterstock: © Africa Studio, 12, © Eldred Lim, 8, © Gelpi JM, 11, © gosphotodesign, 13, © Julie DeGuia, 17, © lsantilli, 4, 21 left, © Mila Semenova, 15, © Olga Lipatova, 18, back cover, © Patricia Chumillas, 6, © Roxana Bashyrova, 14, 20 right, © saisnaps, 7, © Torsak Thammachote, 10, 21 right.

Cover photograph reproduced with permission of Getty Images, E+/Maria Pavlova.

Every effort has been made to contact copyright holders of material reproduced in this book. Any omissions will be rectified in subsequent printings if notice is given to the publisher.

ABERDEENSHIRE LIBRARIES	
3148733	
Bertrams	05/09/2014
J612.86	£11.99

Contents

What can I smell?

I smell cupcakes.

They smell **sweet**.

I smell rotten food.

It smells stinky.

I smell bread.

It smells yummy.

I smell dirty shoes.

They smell stinky.

I smell popcorn.

It smells yummy.

I smell flowers.

They smell sweet.

I smell a wet dog.

It smells stinky.

I smell soap.

It smells **fresh**.

Quiz: Spot the difference

Which of these objects
smells sweet?

Flowers and cupcakes smell sweet.
Wet dogs and dirty shoes smell stinky.

Picture glossary

 **fresh**

 **sweet**

Index

Notes for teachers and parents

BEFORE READING

Building background:
Ask children about their favourite smell. Then ask children what smells are not so nice. How do children smell things? Do they think everyone likes the same smells?

AFTER READING

Recall and reflection:
What smells are from the kitchen (cupcakes, bread)?
What could they smell in the garden (flowers)?

Sentence knowledge:
Ask children to look at page 20. What kind of puncuation is used at the end of the sentence? Why is it there?

Word knowledge (phonics):
Encourage children to point at the word *smell* on page 5. Sound out the four phonemes in the word *s/m/e/l*. Ask the children to sound out each phoneme as they point at the letters and then blend the sounds together to make the word *smell*. Challenge them to say some words that begin with *sm* (small, smart, smash).

Word recognition:
Ask children to point at the word *stinky* on page 7.
Where else can they find the word in the book (page 11)?

EXTENDING IDEAS

Children might enjoy doing a "smell test" at home. Ask them to work with their parents to gather items to smell while blindfolded, such as onions, vinegar, bananas, and ginger. Can they identify the objects by smell? Which smells are their favourites?

In this book

Topic

smell and senses

High-frequency words

a

I

it

they

Sentence stems

1. I smell _____.

2. They smell _____.

3. I _____ a _____.